Pets Need Scrap

MW00682266

A Start-to-Finish Guide for Creating
A Lasting Memory of Your Family Pet

Amber Russell

Amber's Albums Publications, Los Alamitos, California

Pets Need Scrapbooks Too!

A Start-to-Finish Guide for Creating A Lasting Memory of Your Family Pet

By Amber Russell

Published by: Amber's Albums Publications
                 P.O. Box 1764
                 Los Alamitos, CA 90720

ISBN 0-9666639-1-8

PRINTED IN HONG KONG

Dedication

To Dan and Nancy Booth, mentors, confidants, and best friends, whose never ending love, praise, and support gave me the confidence to continue writing and publishing and whose ability to love a pet like their own child provided the inspiration for this book.

Pets add so much to our lives;
it's wonderful to have a small token
to remember them by.

i
n
t
r
o
d
u
c
t
i
o
n

What's In This Book, How To Use It, and Why I Wrote It

Important! If you have never created a scrapbook before and picked up this book because you want to create one that focuses on your pet(s), stop and pick up the telephone to call me to order *Scrapbooking With Amber*, a complete guide that is a must for novice scrapbookers (it also includes a number of page ideas for pets). There are certain things you need to know before you begin creating your first scrapbook to ensure that your end product is something that you will enjoy for years to come. After you have called me (877-700-3161 toll-free), resume reading this introduction.

I have written this book with a single objective in mind: to help you create a scrapbook that captures the essence of what your pet(s) has brought to you and your family's life. We love our pets like a member of the family, yet we neglect to document and remember their lives. Unfortunately, I did not discover the importance of this until I lost one of my dogs to old age and could not find a single picture of her. It was difficult because she and I had literally grown up together, so I vowed at that moment to never let that happen again. Please learn from my experience and start taking pictures of your pet whenever you are taking pictures of your family.

WHAT YOU'LL FIND IN THIS BOOK

The scrapbook that this book is based on was created as a Christmas gift for one of my favorite people, Nancy Booth, who is also my soon-to-be mother-in-law. She and her husband, Dan, have this incredible black labrador named Aberdeen Angus, who is named after a type of cow that Nancy grew up with on her family's dairy farm. Aberdeen is no ordinary dog. He goes on vacation with Nancy and Dan and even sleeps on their bed. He is the reason why restaurants call a to-go container a "doggy bag." He gets nervous when people argue and knows which toy to grab when you say "get your hamburger." As you can see, he's special which is why I decided that making a scrapbook of him would be the best gift for Nancy.

About half of the photos used in the scrapbook were given to me by Dan, and I took the other half myself at different outings and on various trips. (I did borrow the cat photos from a friend because we just lost our cat.) I then organized the photos in chronological order as best I could. Once the photos were in order, I grouped them according to theme. While most of the photos could fit on one page, some required a double-page spread. A double-page spread extends across both pages when a scrapbook is open and can accompany up to six photos.

On the left page of the single-page layouts, you will find a list of the supplies that I used as well as step-by-step instructions for how to recreate that page using your own photos and materials. On the right side of the page, you will find a full-color photo of the actual page that I created for Nancy's scrapbook. For double-page spread layouts (layouts that cover two pages for one theme), you will find full-color photos on both pages with a list of supplies used listed on the left and instructions to follow on the right.

FINAL WORDS

After you have had a chance to read and to begin implementing this book, after you have created a few pages and experienced the excitement, contact me to let me know how you are doing. I want to share your joy and congratulate you for all of your work and dedication. I love to hear good news! My e-mail address is ascrapper@aol.com and my mailing address is P.O. Box 1764, Los Alamitos, CA 90720.

Happy scrapbooking . . .

Step-By-Step Guide to ~~Creating~~ a Family Pet Scrapbook

Helpful hints I've learned along the way to help you get started:

- Stand up when using the circle cutter to stabilize the tool.

- Buy a circle cutter and a template (measurements) to save time.

- Always practice on an extra photo before using any new tool, especially the circle cutter and fancy scissors.

- Use letter stickers or fancy writing for titling to add a finished look.

- Always include dates and places; our memories are only temporary.

- The term "crop" means to cut a photo or paper to a certain size, and "mat" means to place paper behind a photo.

- Always get double prints of your photos. It usually does not cost any extra.

- Use a pet eye pen to remove the white glare often seen in pets' eyes in photos

* I left a great deal of white space on each page to allow Nancy to journal, a form of writing that provides details of the event, including the names of everyone in the photo, dates, and memorable occurrences. Don't skip this valuable step. It will mean so much to you in years to come.

It's A Boy!

Supplies

- Baby bear sticker (Provo Craft®)
- ABC stickers (Provo Craft®)
- Baby rattle sticker (Provo Craft®)
- Baby giraffe sticker (Provo Craft®)
- Pastel striped print paper (Hot Off the Press™)
- Pastel blue paper
- Stork die cut (Creative Memories®)
- Pastel blue brush pen
- Circle cutter

Instructions

Select a puppy photo (or kitten for cat owners) and cut it into a circle with the cutter set at 1/2". Mat it with a circle cut at 3/4" from the striped paper. Place the stork die cut on the right side and the puppy photo over the left edge of the stork's bag. Place the "B" sticker in the upper right corner and the "A" and "C" stickers overlapping it. Angle the rattle sticker on top of the stork's bag. At the bottom of the page by the stork's feet, place the giraffe sticker. Add the bear holding an "A" sticker in the lower left corner; write "It's a boy! (or girl!) at the top and the name of the pet at the bottom. Additional information about how you acquired your pet could also be added to this page.

Supplies

- Sheep stickers (Cherished Memories™ Baby Girl!)
- Sleeping moon stickers (Cherished Memories™ Baby Girl!)
- Lamb & balloon sticker (Provo Craft®)
- Teddy bear sticker (Provo Craft®)
- Cloud paper
- White paper
- Corner rounder

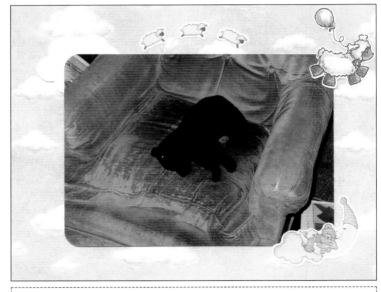

Double-Page Spread

Counting

Sheep

Instructions

Crop the cloud paper to cover both pages completely. Round the corners of two photos of your pet sleeping. Freehand cut two small clouds from white paper and place them under the upper left and lower right corners of the photos. Place three lamb stickers in an arch above each photo and the bear sleeping on the moon sticker on the lower right and upper left corner of each photo. Add the lamb with the ballon and the bear in his pajamas stickers.

Supplies

- Paw print stickers (Provo Craft®)
- Candy heart stickers (Mrs. Grossman's™)
- This Must Be Puppy Love sticker (Melissa Neufeld, Inc.)
- Paw print paper (Provo Craft®)
- Black paper
- Red paper
- Large heart punch (Marvy Uchida)
- Circle cutter
- Corner rounder

Double-Page Spread

This Must Be

Puppy Love!

Instructions

Crop two photos, round corners, mat with black paper, and mount in the upper and lower left corners of each page. Cut two circles from photos at 1/4", matted with paw print paper cut at 1/2", and place over the upper right corner of the left-page photo and the lower right corner of the right-page photo. Punch a heart from red paper for the right page. Place the heart stickers in the upper and lower left corners. Add the paw stickers across both pages and the "This must be puppy love!" sticker.

Supplies

- Butterfly stickers (Provo Craft®)
- Flower stickers (Provo Craft®)
- Winnie the Pooh character stickers (Michael & Co.)
- Pastel blue paper
- Pastel green paper
- Lavender pen
- Pastel green brush pen
- Corner rounder

"The most wonderful wonder is friends."
–Winnie the Pooh

Double-Page Spread

Best

Instructions

Crop four photos and mat one with pastel blue and one with pastel green paper. Draw grass across the bottom of both pages with the green brush pen. Place the Eeyore and Piglet stickers on the left page and Pooh and Tigger stickers on the right page so that they are just touching the grass. Add the flower and butterfly stickers. In the upper left corner, write "The most Wonderful Wonder is friends" quote.

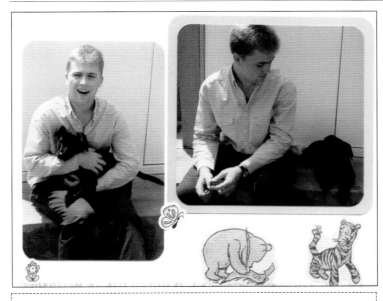

Friends

Chewing Shoes

Supplies

- "My Dog" dog sticker (Provo Craft®)
- Paw prints stickers (Provo Craft®)
- Tennis shoe die cut (Creative Memories®)
- Royal blue paper

Instructions

Select a photo of your puppy chewing something, crop it, and place it in the lower right corner. In the upper left corner, place a cutout photo of your puppy. Cut a bite mark on the lower photo, just below the puppy's mouth. Place a blue piece of paper behind the shoe die cut so the blue shows through and place it in the lower left corner, slightly behind the photo. Just above the shoe die cut, add four paw print stickers. Finish by placing the "My Dog" sticker with his paws resting on top of the lower photo.

I Love School

Supplies

- "I Love School" sticker (Provo Craft®)
- Chalkboard sticker (Mrs. Grossman's™)
- Apple sticker (Mrs. Grossman's™)
- Frog sticker (Mrs. Grossman's™)
- Dog sticker (Mrs. Grossman's™)
- Book sticker (Mrs. Grossman's™)
- Pencil sticker (Mrs. Grossman's™)
- Sunglasses sticker (Mrs. Grossman's™)
- School days print paper (?)
- Corner rounder

Instructions

Crop a photo of your pet near school-related materials. Round the corners of the photo and mat with the school days printed paper. Mount the matted photo in the center at the top of the page. Place the chalkboard sticker in the lower left corner with the frog sticker on the chalk tray and the apple sticker on top of the chalkboard. Add the dog sticker in the lower right corner. Place the book sticker between his paws and the pencil just in front of his paws. Cut out the lenses of the sunglasses sticker before removing the sticker from its backing (use a swivel Ex-acto knife) and then place it over the dog's eyes. Finish by adding the "I Love School" sticker in the center.

Supplies

- Paw print stickers (Provo Craft®)
- Camera sticker (Mrs. Grossman's™)
- Camera tripod sticker (Mrs. Grossman's™)
- Camera flash stickers (Mrs. Grossman's™)
- Black corner stickers (Mrs. Grossman's™)
- Black letter stickers (Creative Memories®)
- Gold paper
- Black pen

Double-Page Spread

Extra!

EXTRA!

about it ...

Extra!

Instructions

Crop two photos of your pet on or near a newspaper. Mat these with gold paper and place in the center of each page. Place the black corner stickers in the outer corner of each page and the paw print stickers in the inner lower corner of each page. Add the camera stickers and place a flash sticker in the upper inside corner of each page. Spell "Extra! Extra!" across the top of each page and write "Read all about it" across the bottom.

Supplies

- Smiling sun sticker (Provo Craft®)
- Playground stickers (Mrs. Grossman's™)
- Teddy bears sticker (Sandylion™)
- Hugging squirrels sticker (Sandylion™)
- Baby chicks sticker (Sandylion™)
- Red letter stickers (Mrs. Grossman's™)
- Puppy die cut (Creative Memories®)
- Red, blue, green, & gold paper
- Circle cutter

Double-Page Spread

Play

Time

Instructions

Cut four circles from photos at 1/2" and mat with blue, red, green, and gold paper cut at 3/4". On the bottom of the left page, place the slide with the bears on top, the wagon, the sandbox with the dog and castle on top, and the truck stickers. Spell "Playtime" down the side and add the sun sticker in the upper right corner. Across the bottom right, place playground and animal stickers and the puppy die cut, with a circle photo just inside his paws.

Having Fun On the Farm

Supplies

- Flower sticker (Provo Craft®)
- Bush with flowers sticker (Mrs. Grossman's™)
- Squirrel sticker (Mrs. Grossman's™)
- Frog stickers (Mrs. Grossman's™)
- Butterfly stickers (Mrs. Grossman's™)
- Hose sticker (Mrs. Grossman's™)
- Water splash stickers (Mrs. Grossman's™)
- Black brush pen
- Corner rounder

Instructions

In the lower left corner, place the bush with flowers sticker. The squirrel sticker goes to the right, then the flower sticker. Round the corners of a photo of your pet playing in the water and mount it in the center of the page. Carefully place the hose sticker so that it is attached to the right side of the page. Add two frog stickers at the bottom and the water splash stickers emerging from the top of the hose. Angle two butterfly stickers to the left of the photo and write "Having fun on (add the place where you took the photo)."

Having fun on

The Farm and the Outdoors

Supplies

- Smiling sun sticker (Provo Craft®)
- Road sticker (Frances Meyer®)
- Tree stickers (Mrs. Grossman's™)
- Truck stickers (Mrs. Grossman's™)
- Bird stickers (Mrs. Grossman's™)
- Black brush pen

Instructions

Cut a strip of the road sticker to fit across the bottom of the page. Cut out a photo of your pet with a toy to place on the road. Add two truck stickers toward the right side of the page. Next to the road, place the bush and the thin tree stickers. Toward the upper left corner, place the large tree sticker with two bird stickers on it. Add the smiling sun sticker in the upper left corner and write "the farm (or wherever you took the photo)" at the top. Randomly place four butterfly stickers.

the farm . . .

Supplies

• Heart sticker (Provo Craft®)
• Dog bone, collar, and tennis ball stickers (Frances Meyer®)
• Paw print sticker strips (Frances Meyer®)
• Blue brush pen

Double-Page Spread

Sticks

and the Park

Instructions

Crop two photos of your pet playing at the park and place in the center of each page. Add the bones, collars, and tennis ball stickers to the corners of the photos. Cut the paw print strip stickers and arrange them down the inside and outside of each page. Write "I Love Sticks and the Park" in blue, making circles at the ends of each letter. Replace the "o" in "love" with the heart sticker.

Supplies

• Flower pot sticker
(Provo Craft®)

• Hunter green, cream,
and brown pattern paper
(Keeping Memories
Alive™ Wilderness
Cottage Collection)

• Pine leaves and cones
frame and label
(Keeping Memories
Alive™ Wilderness
Cottage Collection)

• Black brush pen

• Circle cutter

• Corner rounder

Double-Page Spread

Best Friend

Instructions

Cut dark green paper to cover the left page. Place the pine cone frame over a photo and mount on the left side. Cut a circle from a photo at 1/2", mat with brown plaid paper cut at 3/4", and mount in the lower right corner. Write your pet's name on the label. Cut the brown plaid paper to cover the right page. Crop a photo, round the corners, mat it with cream paper, and place it in the center. Add the flowers in the pot sticker in the lower left corner.

Supplies

• Dream bubbles rub-on transfer (Provo Craft®)
• Dog bowl rub-on transfer (Provo Craft®)
• Dog and puppy stickers (Mrs. Grossman's™)
• Furniture stickers (Mrs. Grossman's™)
• Clock, flower vase, television, and basket of yarn stickers (Mrs. Grossman's™)
• Rope chew sticker (Mrs. Grossman's™)
• Corner rounder

Double-Page Spread

Couch

Potato

Instructions

Round corners of two photos of your pet relaxing and mount them in the center, at the top of each page. On the left page, place the rug sticker first, then the furniture stickers, and then the dog stickers (the puppy goes on the T.V.). Add the clock and vase of flowers stickers. On the right page, add three more dog stickers and the basket of yarn. Put the rope chew sticker inside the dog's paws. The rub-on transfers of the dream bubbles and the dog dish go above the dog's head.

Supplies

• Sun sticker (Provo Craft®)

• Cloud stickers (Frances Meyer®)

• Raccoon, lantern, cooler, blue tea set, fire, & marshmallow stickers (Mrs. Grossman's™)

• Boat, bear, fishing tackle, & fish stickers (Mrs. Grossman's™)

• Tan paper (Making Memories™ Woodland)

• Green and blue paper

• Black pen

• Scallop scissors

• Corner rounder

Double-Page Spread

Mansfield Hollow

Fishing in

Reservoir

Connecticut

Instructions

Cut a hill from green paper for the left page and a lake from blue paper using the scallop scissors for the right. Round corners of two swimming photos matted with tan paper and put them in the center at the top. Place the camping and raccoon sticker on the left page and the fishing stickers on the right. Cut the bottom of the bear's legs so he sits in the boat. Draw the fishing line to the bobber; add the clouds and sun stickers. Write the lake's name in black.

Supplies

• Bubble stickers (Provo Craft®)
• Farm, hay, and grain stickers (Mrs. Grossman's™)
• Tractor, squirrel, grass, and milk can stickers (Mrs. Grossman's™)
• Cow hole punch (Marvy Uchida)
• Cow print paper (Provo Craft®)
• Blue and black paper
• Silver pen (Zig® Opaque Writer)
• Corner rounder

Double-Page Spread

Summer

Vacation

Instructions

Cover 3/4 of each page with light blue paper and the remaining 1/4 with black paper. Round corners of two photos and place toward the center. Place grass stickers across the bottom. Add the farm and milking equipment stickers and the squirrel sticker in the driver's seat of the tractor. Punch cow shapes from black and cow print paper and glue them in the open space. Write the vacation's location with the silver pen and add the bubble stickers.

Picnic

Supplies

- Nesting bird sticker (Provo Craft$^{®}$)
- Insect stickers (Mrs. Grossman's™)
- Barbeque sticker (Mrs. Grossman's™)
- Hamburger and ketchup stickers (Mrs. Grossman's™)
- Grasshopper sticker (Mrs. Grossman's™)
- Grass stickers (Mrs. Grossman's™)
- Red gingham paper (The Paper Patch®)
- Red brush pen
- Black pen
- Corner rounder

Instructions

Crop a picnic or park photo and round the corners. Mat with red gingham paper and mount to the right of center. Across the bottom, place the strips of grass stickers. Add the grill and the grasshopper stickers. Place the ketchup and spatula stickers in the grasshopper's pinchers and the hamburger on the end of the spatula. Arrange the insect and nesting bird stickers around the edges of the photo. Write "Picnic" with the red brush pen, making circles at the ends of each letter. Draw two small loops on various sides of the letters with the black pen.

Party

Supplies

- Cupcake sticker (Provo Craft®)
- Pastel balloon bunch sticker (Provo Craft®)
- Clown parts stickers (Mrs. Grossman's™)
- Ballon stickers (Mrs. Grossman's™)
- PARTY letter stickers (Mrs. Grossman's™)
- Colored dot stickers (Mrs. Grossman's™)
- Polk-a-dot print paper (Creative Memories®)
- Black pen
- Corner rounder

Instructions

Crop a party photo and round the corners. Mat with polk-a-dot print paper and mount in the center, at the bottom of the page. Arrange the clown parts stickers so that the clown is doing a cartwheel across the top of the photo. Spell "PARTY" in the upper left corner with the letter stickers and add various colored dot stickers. Place three balloon stickers in the upper right corner with the middle one slightly higher than the other two. Draw strings with a black pen. Add the cupcake sticker in the lower left corner and the group of ballon sticker in the lower right corner. Be sure to write the name of the event as well as the date.

PARTY

Morgan's
B-day 6/97

True Love

Supplies

• Heart plant stickers (Provo Craft®)
• Lip kiss stickers (Provo Craft®)
• "You May Have to Kiss a Lot of Toads. . ."
sign sticker (Provo Craft®)
• Red heart print paper (Memories
Forever™)
• Red heart frame die cut (Memories
Forever™)

Instructions

Cover the entire page with the red heart print paper. Place the red heart frame over a photo and center them at the bottom of the page. Add the heart flower stickers on either side of the heart. Place the "You May Have To Kiss A Lot of Toads Before You Find Your Handsome Prince" sign sticker in the center, at the top of the page. Finish by adding a lip sticker on each side of the sign sticker.

Vacation at Joshua Tree

Supplies

- "Vacation" sign sticker (Provo Craft®)
- Cactus stickers (Frances Meyer®)
- Horse shoe stickers (Frances Meyer®)
- Cowboy hat sticker ((Frances Meyer®)
- Kokopelli sticker (Mrs. Grossman's™)
- Coyote and cow skull stickers (Hambly™)
- Sun clip art (*Clip Art for Spring and Summer* from Carson-Dellosa Publishing Company)
- Sand colored paper (Memories Forever™)
- Black and yellow brush pen
- Light box (not necessary)

Instructions

Freehand draw and cut sand dunes from tan paper and mount across the bottom of the page. (I made two separate dunes and overlapped them.) Cut out a photo of your pet and place it slightly behind one of the dunes and add a cowboy hat sticker. Place the cactus stickers in the valleys and the horseshoe stickers near the bottom. Arrange the cow skull and coyote metallic stickers so they aren't next to each other. Add the Kokopelli sticker in the center at the bottom. Trace the sun clip art in the upper left corner using a light box or a glass table with a light under it. Fill in with a yellow brush pen. Add the "Vacation" sign sticker in the upper right corner and write the name of your destination with a black brush pen.

Home Sweet Home

Supplies

- Dog house and bones sticker
(Provo Craft®)
- Dog bone die cut (Memories Forever™)
- Fire hydrant die cut (Memories Forever™)
- Paw print paper (Provo Craft®)
- Black pen
- Corner rounder

Instructions

Crop a photo of your pet at home and round the corners; mat with paw print paper and mount just to the left of center on the page. Place the dog bone die cut across the upper left corner of the photo at a 45° angle. Write the name of your pet on the bone die cut with a black pen, making circles at the ends of each letter. Place the fire hydrant die cut in the lower right corner and write "home" on it with a black pen, making circles at the ends of each letter. Finish by adding the dog in his dog house sticker in the lower left corner. Be careful not to cover up the names of those in the photo (like I did).

Thanksgiving

Supplies

• Metallic leaves die cuts (Z-Barten Productions)
• Metallic turkey die cut (Z-Barten Productions)
• Gold paint marker (Current® Inc.)
• Corner rounder

Instructions

Arrange four metallic leaf die cuts so that the top of each leaf is pointing to its respective corner. (You will have to use two of the same color, so be sure to put them across from each other.) Select a photo of your pet at Thanksgiving, crop it, and round the corners. Mount it in the center. Add the tiny metallic turkey die cut to the left of the photo and the tiny metallic leaf die cut to the right. Write "Thanksgiving + the year" with a gold pen across the top of the page.

Supplies

- Dog bone rub-on transfers (Provo Craft®)
- Metallic ornament stickers (Sandylion™)
- Red letter and bow stickers (Mrs. Grossman's™)
- Present stickers (Creative Memories®)
- Ornament die cuts (Creative Memories®)
- Green gingham paper (The Paper Patch®)
- Red & green paper
- Border ruler (Dèjá Views™ by C-Thru®)
- Red and green pens

Double-Page Spread

Christmas

1997

Instructions

Cut two photos into 3/4" circles. Mat one with red paper and the other with green cut at 1". Put green paper behind the green gingham ornament die cut and green gingham paper behind the red and mount according to the example. Add bow stickers at the tops. Draw a red and green line across the top using the border ruler and "hang" ornament stickers from them. Layer present stickers on the bottom inside corners with the dog bone rub-on transfers. With red metallic stickers, spell "Christmas" down the left page and "the year" down the right.

Opening Balloon Present

Supplies

- Holly rub-on transfers (Provo Craft®)
- Red bow sticker (Mrs. Grossman's™)
- Mickey & Minnie print Christmas paper (Hot Off the Press™)
- White paper
- Red pen
- Corner rounder

Instructions

Select a holiday photo of your pet opening a present; crop it and round the corners. Mat it first with white paper so only a 1/4" inch of white can be seen. Then, mat it again with the Micky and Minnie Christmas print paper. Place the photo in the center of the page and add a large red bow sticker at an angle to the upper left corner. In each corner of the page, place a holly leaves and berries rub-on transfer. Be sure to write the date in one of the corners of the page with the red pen.

Easter Egg Hunt

Supplies

- Large bunny sticker (Provo Craft®)
- Baby chick stickers (Provo Craft®)
- Hatching egg stickers (Provo Craft®)
- Carrot sticker (Provo Craft®)
- Easter egg sticker (Provo Craft®)
- Easter basket die cut (Creative Memories®)
- Lavender brush pen

Instructions

Select a photo of your pet on Easter, preferably hunting for eggs (as Aberdeen is pictured here). Cut out the photo and place it in the lower right corner with a chick sticker sitting on top. Place the large bunny sticker near the center (cut the ears off and rearrange them if you need to) with the carrot sticker near his mouth and the chick sticker above his left ear. Place the hatching eggs stickers over the bunny's left leg and the basket die cut over the bottom of the egg stickers. In the lower left corner, add the dyed Easter egg sticker. Finish by writing "easter Egg Hunt + year" in lavender, making circles at the ends of each letter and loops on each side. Write a short caption in the lower left corner.

A Floral Frame

Supplies

- Butterfly stickers (Provo Craft®)
- Little girl offering flower sticker (Provo Craft®)
- Micro flower stickers (Mrs. Grossman's™)
- Circle cutter

Instructions

Cut a circle from a photo with the circle cutter set at 3/4". Make a floral circle around the photo with the mini flower stickers, varying the color and the direction of the flower. Add flower cluster stickers in each corner and two butterfly stickers on opposite sides. Complete the page by adding the child offering a flower sticker in the lower right corner.

Flower Garden

Supplies

- "Garden" sign sticker (Provo Craft®)
- Flower stickers (Mrs. Grossman's™)
- Grass stickers (Mrs. Grossman's™)
- Watering can die cut (Creative Memories®)
- Yellow brush pen
- Blue pen
- Corner rounder

Instructions

Crop a photo, round the corners, and mount in the center, 1/2" from the bottom of the page. Over the upper right corner of the photo, place the watering can die cut at an angle. Draw water drops with the blue pen. Cut 1" strips of the grass stickers (while the backing is still on) and place on each side of the photo, flush with the bottom of the page. Add a yellow and pink flower sticker to the center of the tufts of grass. Hang the "garden" sign sticker in the center at the top of the page and draw a sun in the upper left corner with the yellow brush pen.

Supplies

- Sun in clouds sticker (Provo Craft®)
- Palm tree sticker (Provo Craft®)
- Crab & starfish stickers (Mrs. Grossman's™)
- Beach gear stickers (Mrs. Grossman's™)
- Water stickers (Mrs. Grossman's™)
- Sand colored paper (Memories Forever™)
- Cloud template (All Night Media®)
- Blue & black brush pens
- Corner rounder

Double-Page Spread

Running on

the Beach

Instructions

Crop two beach photos, round corners, and mount at an angle toward the top of each page. Place a piece of sand-colored paper over the photos for the beach and strips of the water stickers across the bottom for the ocean. Put the beach, sea life, and palm tree stickers on the sand and the clouds and sun sticker in the upper right corner on the left page. Trace the cloud template across the top of both pages and write the name of the beach in black pen.

Sunflower Silhouette

Supplies

- Sunflower printed paper (The Paper Patch®)
- White paper
- Corner rounder

Instructions

Cut the sunflower paper to cover the entire page. Crop a photo, round the corners, and mat with white paper. Mount the matted photo in the center of the page. Keep in mind that you can change the printed paper to match whatever flower or background that is in your photo.

I Love Cats

Supplies

- "I Love Cats" sticker (Provo Craft®)
- Bird house sticker (Provo Craft®)
- Cat sticker (Provo Craft®)
- Deep red paper
- Tan paper (Making Memories™ Woodland colors)
- Corner punch (Marvy Uchida)

Instructions

Cover the entire page with the tan paper. Select a photo of your pet and round the corners with the special corner punch. Use the corner punch on the deep red paper and use for a mat for the photo. Mount the two in the center, 1/4" from the bottom of the page. Place the birdhouse sticker in the bottom left corner and the surprised cat sticker in the lower right corner. Finish by placing the "I Love Cats" sticker in the center at the top of the page.

Dreaming of Fish

Supplies

- Fish in bowl rub-on transfer (Provo Craft®)
- Cat in fish bowl sticker (Provo Craft®)
- Dream bubble stickers (Provo Craft®)
- Fish print paper (Provo Craft®)
- Pool water print paper (Creative Memories®)
- Circle cutter

Instructions

Cover the page with the fish print paper. Select a photo of your pet in the sink (or near water or a fish bowl) and cut it with the circle cutter set at 3/4". Mat the photo with the pool water print paper cut at 1". Mount the matted photo in the center, 1/4" from the bottom of the page. Place a bubbles sticker to the left of the photo, preferably near the pet's head. Just above the bubbles, place the fish bowl rub-on transfer. Finish by adding the cat with his paw in the fish bowl sticker in the lower right corner.

Sunning Myself

Supplies

- Napping cat sticker (Provo Craft®)
- Shining sun sticker (Provo Craft®)
- Blue marble print paper (Cherished Memories™)
- Corner rounder

Instructions

Cover the entire page with the blue marble print paper. Crop a photo of your pet relaxing in the sun and round the corners. Place it in the center, 1/4" from the bottom of the page. Over the upper left corner of the photo, add the shining sun sticker. Finish by covering the upper right corner of the photo with the napping cat sticker.

You Caught Me

Supplies

- Paw print stickers (Provo Craft®)
- Black paper
- Corner rounder

Instructions

Cover the entire page with a piece of black paper. Crop a memorable photo of your pet and round the corners. Mount the photo in the center of the page. Over each corner of the photo, place a paw print sticker. If you would like to journal on this page, use a silver or gold opaque writing pen so it will stand out against the black background.

**c
o
n
c
l
u
s
i
o
n**

Congratulations!

I begin every one of my conclusions with that expression because I know the incredible amount of time and dedication it takes to complete any type of project, especially a scrapbook. With the hustle and bustle of everyday life, I'm impressed by anyone who can see the importance of preserving memories and make the time for it. You did it and now you have a priceless treasure to share with your friends and family for years to come. You will never find yourself in the position I was in a few years ago when I had no photos of the pet that I grew up with and no way to share of all my memories of our fun times together. Pets add so much to our lives, and it's wonderful to have a small token to remember them by. In your hands (or those of someone admiring your work) is a one-of-a-kind keepsake that is destined for the coffee table.

Although this scrapbook focuses on your family pet(s), there are many more scrapbooks in you. In this book, I have provided you with the information to create a complete scrapbook, and that concept can be used for any subject that deserves remembering. You can now move on to create many scrapbooks, possibly of another pet, or a wedding, or a gift for a favorite friend. Whatever your next project is I would like to hear about it and share in your excitement. It is important to me to know that you created a pet scrapbook because of this book and then moved on to create many more. You can write to me at the address on the inside cover of the book, or you can e-mail me at ascrapper@aol.com. I truly look forward to hearing from you.

Don't forget that you are the only one who notices any of the mistakes you may have made while creating your scrapbook. There are a couple of sticker/tape removing products out on the market that you can use to remove a sticker and die cut. Take advantage of this if you spell something incorrectly or make any other "major" mistake. Otherwise, allow the small imperfections to add originality to your scrapbook. And besides, my bet is that no one else will even notice them! They will be too busy praising you for your creativity.

ABOUT THE AUTHOR

Surrounded by a stack of essays, a table full of scrapbooking supplies, and an eager five-year-old, Amber Russell sits at her computer, working on her next how-to scrapbook guide. Although she is a full-time high school English and journalism teacher and a single parent, she makes the time to preserve her family's memories by taking thousands of photos and bringing them to life in scrapbooks.

She strongly believes that every child deserves to have access to his/her family's heritage in order to build a stronger family unit and sense of history. She wrote her first book, *Scrapbooking With Amber*, with that concept in mind. *Pets Need Scrapbooks Too!* was her next project because of the importance of a family pet to the family unit; in fact, she just adopted a black labrador puppy as this book went to print. She finds her daily motivation in the words of J. Goddard: "Happiness is the art of making a bouquet of those flowers within reach."

The following companies make the products I used to create my scrapbook. Most of the products are sold at your local craft or scrapbook store. Call for the location of the store nearest you that carries their product.

All Night Media®
(415) 459-3013

The C-Thru Ruler Co.®
(860) 243-0303

Creative Memories®
(800) 468-9335

Current®, Inc.
(719) 594-4100

D.J. Inkers™
(801) 565-0894

EK Success Ltd. (Zig Pens®)
(201) 939-5404

Frances Meyer, Inc.®
(912) 748-5252

Hambly Studios, Inc.™
(408) 496-1100

Hot Off the Press™
(503) 266-9102

Keeping Memories Alive™
(800) 419-4949

Making Memories
(801) 295-8500

Mellissa Neufeld, Inc.
(800) 638-3353

Mello Smello®
(Cherished Memories™)
(612) 504-5400

Michael & Company
Culver City, CA

Memories Forever™
Western Trimming Corp.
(818) 998-8550

Mrs. Grossman's Stickers™
(800) 429-4549

The Paper Patch®
(800) 397-2737

Provo Craft®
(800) 937-7686

Sandylion™
(905) 475-0523

Uchida of America
(800) 541-5877

Z-Barten Productions
(310) 202-7070

index

ORDER FORM

✳ Fax orders: (877) 700-3161 (toll free)

☎ Telephone orders: Call (877) 700-3161 (toll free). Have your Visa or MasterCard ready.

▣ Postal orders: Send check or money order to Amber's Albums, P.O. Box 1764, Los Alamitos, CA 90720, USA

Please send a copy of _____ to:

Name: _____

Address: _____

City: _____

State: _____

Zip: _____

Telephone: (____) _____

Sales tax:
Please add 7.75% for books shipped to California addresses.
Shipping:
$4.00 for the first book and $2.00 for each additional book.

Payment:
❏ Check
❏ Credit Card: ❏ Visa   ❏ MasterCard

Card number: _____

Name on card: _____   Exp.date: _____

Signature _____